Piero Ventura

VENICE

Birth of a City

G.P. Putnam's Sons

NEW YORK

Originally published in Italy by Fabbri Editori, 1987,
under the title *Venezia, nascita di una città*.
English translation/adaptation by John Grisewood.
Printed and bound in Italy by Sagdos, Brugherio, Milano.
Book design by Martha Rago
First Impression December 1987

Library of Congress Cataloging-in-Publication Data
Ventura, Piero. Venice, birth of a city.
Summary: Traces the history of the city built on
islands in the Adriatic Sea from its establishment
in A.D. 452 to the height of its political and economic
power as a colonial empire and cultural center in the
1400's to its conquest by Napoleon in 1797.
Translation of: Venezia, nascita di una città.
1. Venice (Italy)—History—Pictorial works—
Juvenile literature. [1. Venice (Italy)—History]
I. Title.   DG676.V4613   1988   945'.31   87-25892
ISBN 0-399-21531-X

Venice is the strangest, most fascinating and perhaps the most beautiful city in the world. It is built on an archipelago of over 110 low islets in the Lagoon of Venice. The islets are protected from the open sea, the Adriatic, by the Lido, a sandbar over 6 miles long.

The magnificent churches and *palazzi* (palaces) of this fairy-tale city are supported by innumerable wooden poles driven into the islets' muddy sediment. La Serenissima—the Most Serene—as Venice came to be called, was a meeting place of East and West and a great trading republic through which passed the riches of Asia. Venetian merchants traveled all over Asia, bringing back with them silks, emeralds, rubies, spices and scents.

So why was this city ever built on swampy islands in the middle of a desolate lagoon? The first Venetians were fishermen, hunters and boatmen who were skilled enough at navigating the maze of muddy banks and shallows to make a living. The real history of the city began in the fifth century. Frightened coastal dwellers fleeing barbarian hordes who poured into Italy after the downfall of the Roman Empire settled on these offshore islands. These refugees had lived in fine Roman cities. Here on the islands they started a new life, for the most part undisturbed by the Lombard invaders on the mainland. They drew closer together and on the Rivo Alto (Rialto), a central lagoon township, Venice grew up.

The Latin name Venetia refers to the whole area of the northern Adriatic; this region was once part of the Roman Empire. In the sixth century it became part of the Byzantine Empire, which had developed from the Eastern Roman Empire, centered at first at Ravenna and later at Constantinople. The Byzantines gradually lost control of Venezia (Venice) and by 697 the people elected their own duke, or doge. The last doge was deposed eleven hundred years later, in 1797. The story of Venice during these years is what we shall look at on the following pages.

The fortunes of Venice have always been linked to the sea from which she sprang. Having no agricultural land to cultivate, the Venetians turned to the sea for their living—from fishing, later from boatbuilding, and from the crystallization of sea salt. The very early fishermen were the first to learn how to "harvest" the highly saline seawater of the lagoon. In the days long before canning and refrigeration, salt was much sought after for preserving meat and fish. And so for the Venetians salt became a valuable commodity, which they traded on the mainland in exchange for grain and wine. Thus it was that the landless Venetians always had full granaries.

Salt, produced from the seawater of the lagoon, was the most important commodity traded by early Venetian merchants.

Saltworks were dotted about all over the lagoon.

A raft of tree trunks is being towed to the shipyard.

Wooden boats were the only means of transport along Venice's streets of water.

The wooden bridge of the Rialto joined the original two principal islands on which Venice grew.

Shipyards were built near people's homes. Whole families worked there.

1000 The Foundation of a Great City—Timber

The buildings of Venice are supported on foundations of millions of larch poles driven into the muddy islets. But Venice was also supported by wood in another important way: shipbuilding. Early in the eleventh century Venice and her great rival city Genoa began a flourishing trade with Asia, and shipbuilding became an essential industry. Timber for the shipyards was felled in the vast coastal forests of Istria, and was then tied into rafts and floated down to Venice.

1271 Venice and the Orient—Marco Polo

By the end of the thirteenth century Venice had become a great
trading city, rivaled by only Genoa and Pisa. Among Venice's many
merchants were two brothers, Nicolò and Matteo Polo. On a
voyage to the East in 1271, Nicolò decided to take his seventeen-
year-old son, Marco, along. Setting sail from Venice, they arrived in
Asia Minor and took the "silk route" across Persia and the vast Gobi
Desert until they reached Peking. There they were welcomed by
Kublai Khan, the Mongol conqueror. The Polos stayed many years
in China, and Marco traveled all over the country in the service of
the Khan. They returned to Venice in 1295.

*The roll call of seamen.
The seated scribe is
ticking off the names.
Behind him stands the
ship's captain.*

Marco Polo's ship ready to weigh anchor. The Polos stayed in China for twenty-four years.

When Marco returned home he wrote down the stories of his travels. Il Milione, *or* The Travels of Marco Polo, *is one of the most exciting books ever written.*

During the fifteenth century Venice won territory on the mainland of Italy. The Venetian Republic was now an established power on land as well as at sea. The fifteenth century was perhaps the most glorious time in Venice's history largely because Venice controlled the sea and therefore water trade-routes to the East. The Venetian ships were built in dockyards called the Arsenal. From 1100 on the Arsenal was efficiently organized into specialized units or departments. One department looked after the sawmills and carpenters' shops where the ships' hulls were built; another oversaw the caulking to make sure the hulls were watertight; and other departments were set up for sailmaking and for manufacturing rope and oars. Dry docks also were located in the Arsenal; here the ships' keels were regularly checked and repaired. In the Arsenal's bakehouse ships' biscuits were made and in the foundries anchors and cannon were cast.

The Arsenal was efficiently organized. In 1570 it took only two months to launch a hundred new galleys to fight the Turks who were attacking the Venetian colony of Cyprus. Shipbuilding was so important to the Venetians that the *arsenalotti*—the dockworkers—were a privileged workforce organized along military lines. The *arsenalotti* were the personal bodyguards of the doge, as well as serving as firefighters. They had the responsibility for keeping public order and for guarding the Mint, where the Venetian gold ducat was made.

An arsenalotto, *or dockworker*

The admiral, the head of the Arsenal

An aerial view of the Arsenal. Here the ships that made La Serenissima great were built. The four great docks are linked together. In dry dock keels were overhauled for any damage caused by the teredo mollusk, a shipworm which attacks the submerged parts of a ship's timbers. Beneath the red roofs are countless slips, or stocks, where ships' hulls were built.

Docks of the newest Arsenal

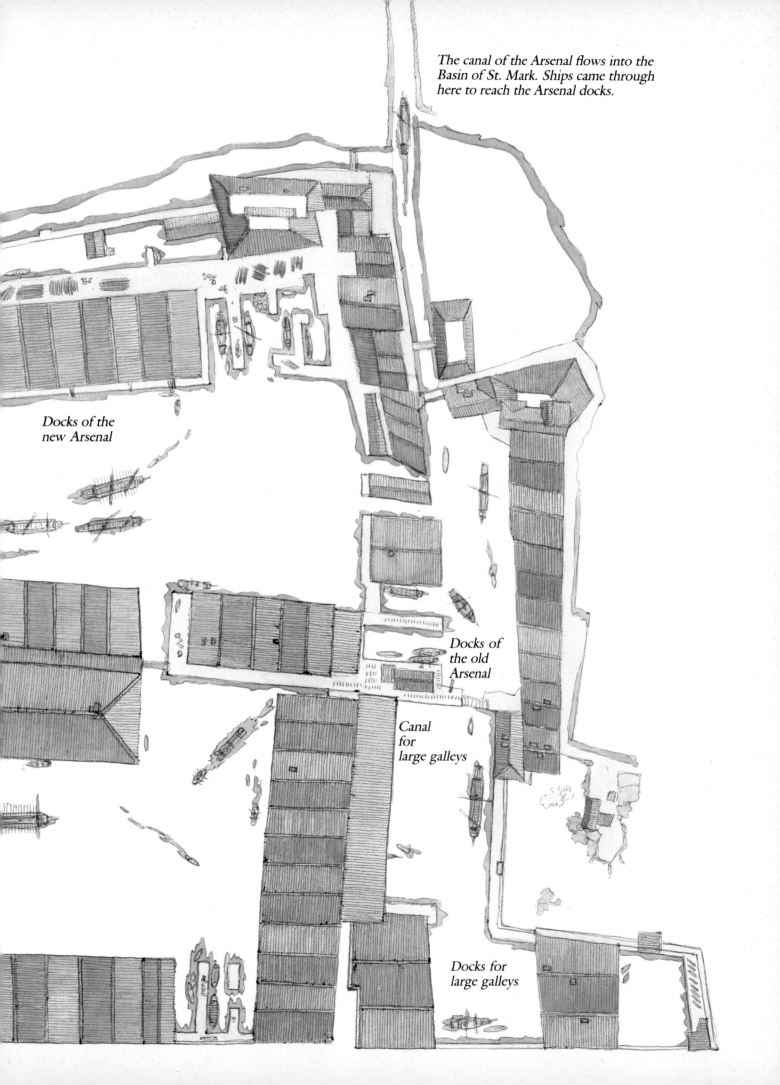

The canal of the Arsenal flows into the Basin of St. Mark. Ships came through here to reach the Arsenal docks.

Docks of the new Arsenal

Docks of the old Arsenal

Canal for large galleys

Docks for large galleys

1400 The Great Galley

By 1400 Venice had obtained islands and trading posts throughout the eastern Mediterranean and had become one of the great states of Europe. These possessions had to be defended from other seafaring powers. A special fighting ship, the Great Galley of Venice, was developed; it was feared all over the Mediterranean. The Great Galley was a mixture of a Venetian merchant craft and a fighting ship, with the best features of both. The solid, slow, round-bottomed merchant ship carried sails and had a pair of rudders; the long, sleek fighting ship had low sides and was propelled at great speed by many pairs of oars. This Great Galley had the solidity of a merchant ship and the fleetness of a fighting ship. It was a most versatile vessel. When loaded with cargo, it was a merchant ship; unloaded, it was a man-of-war. Unlike other ships of the day, the Venetian Great Galley did not use galley slaves as oarsmen. Instead the oarsmen were free men who traded and carried arms. This meant that when the ship was attacked the whole crew took part in fighting off the enemy, making a Venetian warship's fighting manpower far greater than that of its rivals.

The Venetian Great Galley could carry 200 tons of cargo, in addition to being armed with cannon. The crew totaled up to 200 seamen.

The Great Lantern, lit during night sailings

The aftercastle, with the captain's quarters

Rudder

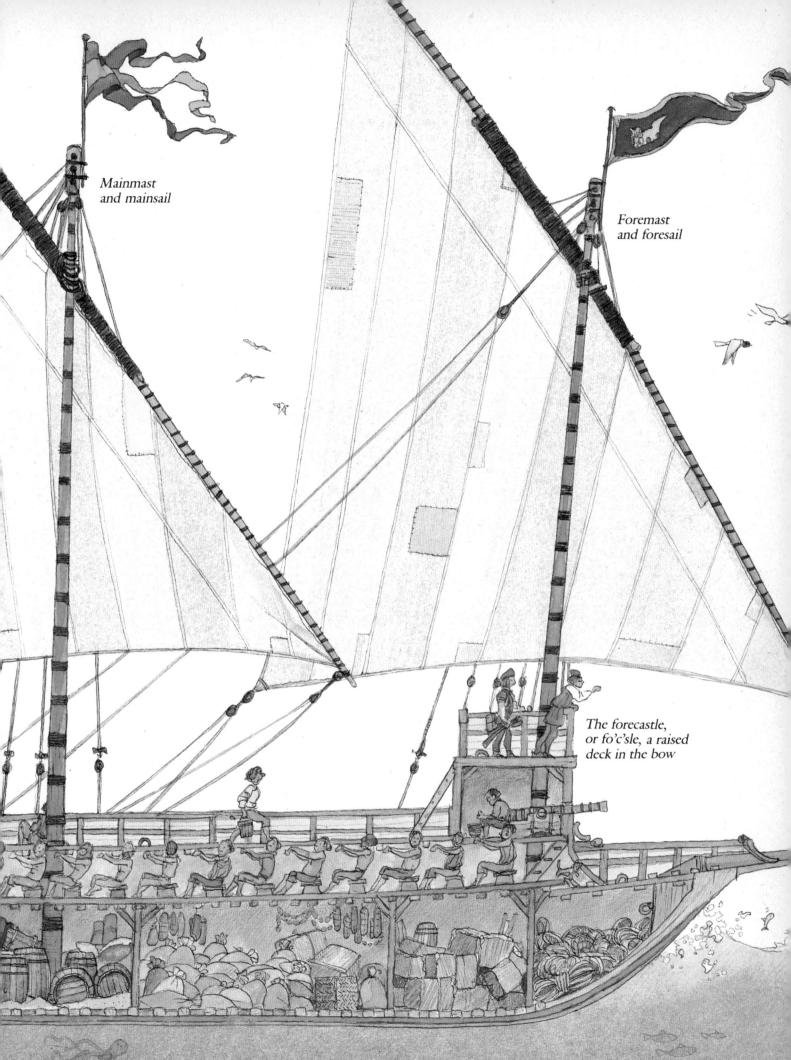

Mainmast
and mainsail

Foremast
and foresail

The forecastle,
or fo'c'sle, a raised
deck in the bow

1400　The Richest City in the World

Throughout the 1300s Venice struggled constantly and bitterly with her greatest rival, Genoa, and in 1379 was almost defeated by the Genoese fleet. The Venetians just managed to force the besieged Genoese to surrender at Chioggia in 1380. In 1347 half of Venice's population was killed by the Black Death (bubonic plague) and in 1382 the plague returned. Added to this there were political revolts. But by 1400 Venice had recovered from this turbulence to become the richest and one of the most powerful states in the world. She won or bought new ports and trading posts and even tried to extend her territory in northern Italy. The Venetians loved trade and the great noble families did not disdain commerce, as nobles in many other countries did. Many families created huge fortunes for themselves through trade. During the Golden Age of the 1400s, the city's revenues were astronomical. And Venice adorned herself with palaces, churches and other monuments of surpassing beauty.

A typical campo, *or small square*

A public gondola

A family gondola. Venetian families vied with each other to see who could have the most luxurious gondola with the handsomest gondolier.

1400 An Aristocratic Republic

Venice's chief citizen or head of state was the doge (or duke). He was elected by the Maggior Consiglio, or Great Council, composed mainly of nobles. From the end of the thirteenth century onward, the doge was little more than a powerless but pampered figurehead, the central figure in the great pageants and ceremonies the Venetians loved. Venice was an *oligarchy* governed

Members of the doge's council accompanying the doge. They were known as scarlatti ("scarlets"), for the color of their robes.

The doge

The 240 Pregadi councillors constituted the government of the Republic, in name at least.

by a few noble families. Real power was invested in the Great Council, which was made up of a thousand nobles. In addition to electing the doge, the Great Council appointed members to all other bodies of the Republic: the Council of Ten, one of the most feared political organizations, which was set up to maintain law and order and which ran its own secret service; the Minor Council, which assisted the doge; and the so-called Council of the Pregadi, a kind of advisory body similar to the British House of Lords.

The Council of the Pregadi met in a vast hall with benches facing each other.

The Venetians loved pageants and processions. This delight in showing off their wealth was also an expression of pride in their city at a time—in the 1500s—when Venice's greatness was beginning to fade. Each year at all the great feasts and festivals the doge's procession went around the city proclaiming Venetian pride and self-importance. Flags bearing the coat of arms of Venice were ceremoniously carried at the head of the procession, symbolizing the city's civic and spiritual unity. The flagbearers were followed by musicians and then by the doge's treasurers and squires. Behind them were the church canons, and then the patriarch, or archbishop, of Venice in pontifical vestments. Behind the patriarch were the deacons and secretaries. Following them were the bearers of the doge's insignia: the white candle; the *"corno,"* or crown; and the *cattedra,* the throne and seat of authority—all symbols of his supreme power. Beneath a damask umbrella walked the doge, His Most Serene Highness himself, wearing a cape of ermine and gold. At the end of the procession were the diplomatic corps, a swordbearer and the nobles of the Republic.

Nobles of the Republic

Canons in sacred vestments

The patriarch, or archbishop, of Venice

Treasurers and squires of the doge

Musicians

wordbearer   *Ambassadors*   *A squire
carrying a
damask umbrella*   *His Most Serene Highness
the Doge*   *Bearers of
the golden throne*

Deacons and secretaries   *Bearer of the
white candle*   *Bearer of the
doge's crown*

Standardbearers

1500 The Artisans of Venice

Venice was a city of merchants largely because it was also a city of skilled artisans. The goods produced by the artisans were traded by the merchants for the spices, scents and emeralds of the Orient. Venetian glassware was world-famous, and mirrors were for a long time made only in Venice. In 1292, because of the fire hazard of their furnaces, the glassmakers were ordered to move to the nearby island of Murano. Venetian woodworkers—cabinetmakers, inlayers and lacquerers—were famous for their beautiful, elaborate furniture. Vast quantities of silk (from the East) and wool (from England) were imported to Venice to be spun and dyed and woven into precious velvets, brocades and damasks. Venetian jewelers produced superb gold and silver jewelry in the Byzantine style. Lacemakers on the island of Burano made one of the most sought-after laces in Europe, the *punto in aria* pattern, which is still made there today. Venetian printers illustrated books with the most sophisticated wood-engraving techniques and covered their books in handsome gold-stamped leather bindings.

Lacemaking pillow and bobbins

Venetian pillow lace

Two master glassmakers blowing molten glass through an iron pipe

A furnace in which the silicate for making glass was melted

Two master glassmakers pulling molten glass to make glass sticks

Naval carpenters, among the highest-paid workers in Venice, making oars for galleys

A cabinetmaker and joiner at work

Priceless materials being dyed in a vat

A press for printing books

The very finest products of the Venetian glassmaker and jeweler

A rare sight—the church of Santa Maria Formosa covered with snow

1500 The City of Art

From the year 1500 Venice was still powerful, but increasingly threatened by the rise of the Ottoman Empire. This was a time of great artistic energy. Architects, sculptors and stonemasons embellished the city, while decorators, plasterers and woodworkers adorned the interiors of churches and palaces. But perhaps Venice's greatest legacy, apart from the city itself, is its painting. Among Venetian painters of the fifteenth and sixteenth centuries are some of the greatest masters of all time: Jacopo Bellini (1400–1470) and his sons, Giovanni and Gentile; Andrea Mantegna (1431–1506); Vittore Carpaccio (before 1460–1525); Giorgione (1478–1511); Titian (1477–1576); Lorenzo Lotto (1480–1556); Paolo Veronese (1528–1588); and Tintoretto (1518–1594), whom you can see at work below.

1500　Venice and the Ottoman Turks

In 1380 Venice had defeated her greatest trading rival—Genoa. But a new and far more menacing rival now threatened Venice from the East: the Ottoman Empire. In 1453 the Ottoman Turks captured Constantinople (now Istanbul, the capital of Turkey). In the following years the Turks harassed Venetian shipping and in 1470 they won an important naval battle at Negroponte in the northern Aegean Sea. This marked the beginning of Venice's long decline. In 1492 Christopher Columbus discovered America, opening up what was to become a vast new market for European traders. In 1497 Vasco da Gama sailed from Portugal on a voyage around Africa's Cape of Good Hope to India. This put an end to Venice's monopoly of the spice trade. In the 1500s Turkish expansion increased in the Mediterranean. Syria was conquered in 1517, Rhodes in 1522. The whole Mediterranean coast from Albania to Morocco was in Ottoman hands. In 1571 Venice joined the Holy League of Christians and defeated the Turks in the great naval battle at Lepanto. Despite their defeat, the Turks managed to seize Cyprus, Venice's stronghold in the eastern Mediterranean. In 1669 Venice lost Crete, her last overseas possession, to the Turks.

During battle sails were furled and the ships were propelled by oarsmen.

Fire aboard an enemy
ship was the quickest
way to victory.

The shipwrecked and
wounded were picked up
only at the end of a battle.

1700 The Grand Canal

The heart of Venice is split in half by what must surely be the world's most spectacular thoroughfare: the Grand Canal. This 1.8-mile-long waterway curves through the city in the shape of a reversed letter *S*. Along its banks are the *palazzi* (palaces or town houses) built by rich families. Most rich families dreamed of building their own *palazzo* overlooking the Grand Canal and 200

A Turkish warehouse, built in the 1200s

Ca' Pesaro, built in the late 1600s, now home of the Gallery of Modern Art

Palazzo Giustinian, built in the 1400s

Ca' Giustinian, built in the 1400s

Palazzo Corner della Ca' Grande, built in the 1500s

Palazzo Grassi, built in the 1700s

Palazzo Grimar built in the late 1500s

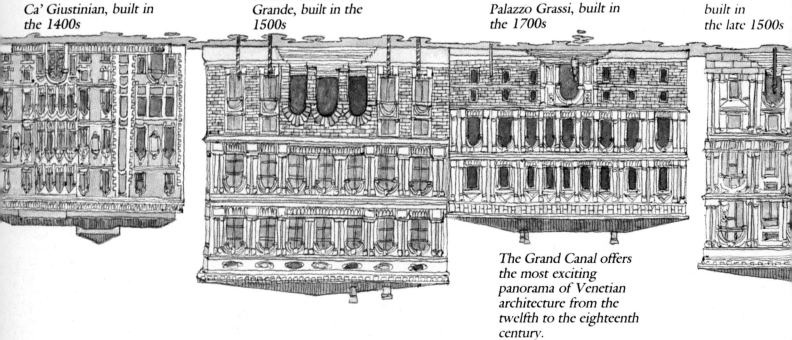

The Grand Canal offers the most exciting panorama of Venetian architecture from the twelfth to the eighteenth century.

such palaces were built between the twelfth and eighteenth centuries. The Grand Canal presents an imposing panorama of architectural styles—Byzantine, Gothic, Lombard, Renaissance, Baroque and Neoclassical. Perhaps the most famous palace is the Ca' d'Oro—the House of Gold—Gothic in style and with a façade painted and decorated in gold. Many of these splendid buildings have become hotels, museums or municipal offices. Some, sadly, are crumbling and deserted.

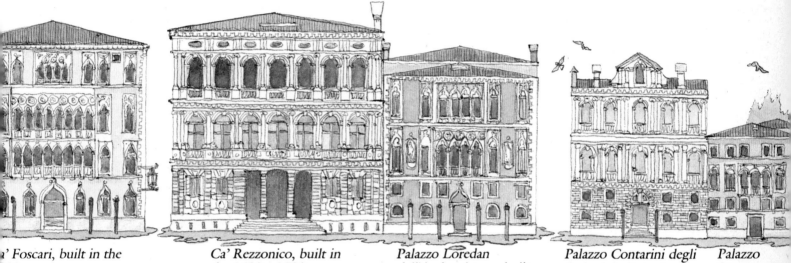

*a' Foscari, built in the
*00s, now
*ministrative center of
e university

*Ca' Rezzonico, built in
the 1600s–1700s, now
the Museum of
Eighteenth-Century
Venice. The poet Robert
Browning lived here for a
time.*

*Palazzo Loredan
dell'Ambasciatore, built
in the 1400s*

*Palazzo Contarini degli
Scrigni, built in the
1600s*

*Palazzo
Querini,
built in
the 1700s*

*Palazzo Bembo, built in
the 1400s*

*Ca' d'Oro, built between
1421 and 1440, the most
famous palace along the
Grand Canal*

*Palazzo Loredan
Vendramin Calergi, built
in the early 1500s*

*Palazzo Correr
Contarini, built in the
1600s*

*All decorations are concentrated on
the façades of the buildings. This was
done to display the owners' wealth
and importance. But the imposing
wide windows and colonnades also
served practical purposes. They
reduced the weight of the walls on the
larch-pole foundations and also
allowed more light into the interiors.*

Masks, pranks, games—
all the fun of Carnival

At carnival time even the
gondolas "wear masks."
The boats are decorated
with ribbons, flowers and
papier-mâché figures.

1700 Carnival

As Venice's power and importance faded during the 1700s, a carefree spirit seemed to invade the city. It became a favorite stopping place for people on the Grand Tour of the ancient monuments of Greece and Rome. Of the lavish galas and extravagant entertainments put on by the Venetians, none was more spectacular than the annual Carnevale, which took place during the week before the penitential season of Lent. Carnival time was a time for feasting, music-making, dancing in the streets and wearing fancy dress. Everyone, nobles and commoners alike, hid behind the famous *bautta,* (the black or white domino mask that covered the eyes). Carnival came to a climax on Shrove Tuesday   outside the Doges' Palace.

Carnival was encouraged by the Venetian Republic and preparations for it were treated as seriously as any other work.

1700 La Fenice Theater

The Venetian love of music and theater of all kinds has a long tradition. During the 1700s the Venetians spent a great deal of time at the theater and at concerts. In 1729 Venice's most famous theater opened—the elegant and sumptuously decorated Teatro La Fenice (The Phoenix). In the seventeenth century in most countries of Europe, music was usually performed only at court; in Venice at that time there were seventeen public theaters. The city was one of the great musical centers of Europe. Among the most famous composers were Claudio Monteverdi (1567–1643), composer of operas, madrigals and masses, and Antonio Vivaldi (1675–1741). Vivaldi taught music to the orphan girls of the Conservatorio della Pietà, who formed one of the girls' choirs for which Venice was famous. Among the playwrights whose works were performed at La Fenice, the comic dramatist Carlo Goldoni (1707–1793) is perhaps the best known.

A scenery painter at work

A chorus master and choristers

The sets and stage effects
became ever more
elaborate.

Musicians in the wings
accompanying a rehearsal
by the performers

Venice's Marriage with the Sea

Every year for over 600 years the doge sailed beyond the Lido into the open sea in his state galley, the Bucintoro, or Bucentaur. This event took place on the religious feast of the Ascension. Aboard the gilded galley were the doge's council, church dignitaries and distinguished guests. The majestic galley, captained by the admiral, head of the Arsenal, was rowed by the *arsenalotti*. When the galley reached the open sea, the doge pronounced these words: "We wed thee, O sea, as a token of our true and everlasting love," and so saying he threw a symbolic wedding ring into the sea. This tradition died with the end of the Republic of Venice in 1797. On May 12 of that year in the Great Council Chamber, the last doge, Ludovico Manin, abdicated to Napoleon. The Republic ceased to exist and Venice was placed under Austrian control by Napoleon. Imperial soldiers looted the city and the doge's ceremonial galley was burned.

Although the Bucintoro was burned, the Venetians rebuilt it. The splendid ceremony of the marriage with the sea is reenacted today.

The Bucintoro never carried masts or sails. Richly adorned with gilded decorations and statues, it was used only on ceremonial occasions.

Venice Today

Although the Venetians revolted against their Austrian overlords in 1848—"the Year of Revolutions"—Venice remained in Austrian hands until 1866, when it became part of the new United Kingdom of Italy. Since then the city has had to face up to new threats: pollution and subsidence. Pollution is caused by the acid fumes that pour out of the factories on the mainland. These eat into the stonework of many buildings. Subsidence—the slow sinking of the city—may well be caused by the extraction of underground gases for use in industry. As Venice has begun to sink, various parts of it become flooded when tides are high. Campaigns to "save Venice" have attracted worldwide attention, and the concern has been so great that money has poured in from many countries. These funds have helped pay for the work done to restore and repair many works of art and architecture, monuments to Venice's great past.

If the pollution hanging over the city is greatly reduced, and if proposed remedies to the sinking of the city have effect, there is hope that Venice will survive to be admired for many more years to come.

Venice Today

Although the Venetians revolted against their Austrian overlords in 1848—"the Year of Revolutions"—Venice remained in Austrian hands until 1866, when it became part of the new United Kingdom of Italy. Since then the city has had to face up to new threats: pollution and subsidence. Pollution is caused by the acid fumes that pour out of the factories on the mainland. These eat into the stonework of many buildings. Subsidence—the slow sinking of the city—may well be caused by the extraction of underground gases for use in industry. As Venice has begun to sink, various parts of it become flooded when tides are high. Campaigns to "save Venice" have attracted worldwide attention, and the concern has been so great that money has poured in from many countries. These funds have helped pay for the work done to restore and repair many works of art and architecture, monuments to Venice's great past.

If the pollution hanging over the city is greatly reduced, and if proposed remedies to the sinking of the city have effect, there is hope that Venice will survive to be admired for many more years to come.

The Bucintoro never carried masts or
sails. Richly adorned with gilded
decorations and statues, it was used
only on ceremonial occasions.